Congratulations! It's a Boy!

God's Gift: A Story of Love

DALE ANTHONY
and
RACHAEL ANTHONY

ISBN 978-1-63575-113-0 (Hard Cover)
ISBN 978-1-63575-112-3 (Digital)

Christian Faith Publishing, Inc.
296 Chestnut Street
Meadville, PA 16335
www.christianfaithpublishing.com

Printed in the United States of America

Congratulations!
It's a Boy!

God's Gift: A Story of Love

A Special Gift For You:

_____

Place Photograph
of Your Baby
Boy Here:

Height: _____

Weight: _____

Birthdate: _____

1

We prayed to God

He answered our prayer

We waited for you

And now you are here

A gift from God

A bundle of joy

A miracle child

Our baby boy

Warming our heart

Comforting our soul

You brought happiness

And made us whole

A promise from heaven

From the Father above

An angel arrived

To show us God's love

We give God thanks

For your precious birth

Heaven came down

To bless us on earth

You entered our world

To brighten our days

To fill us with love

In so many ways

12

13

Your sparkling eyes

Your soft tender touch

Deeply remind us

Why we love you so much

Whenever you smile

We smile with you

You are so special

That's why we love you

To hold you in our arms

To hear your lovely voice

You amaze us with your charms

Together we rejoice

God's blessings be on you

God give you all you need

God guide and direct you

In thought and word and deed

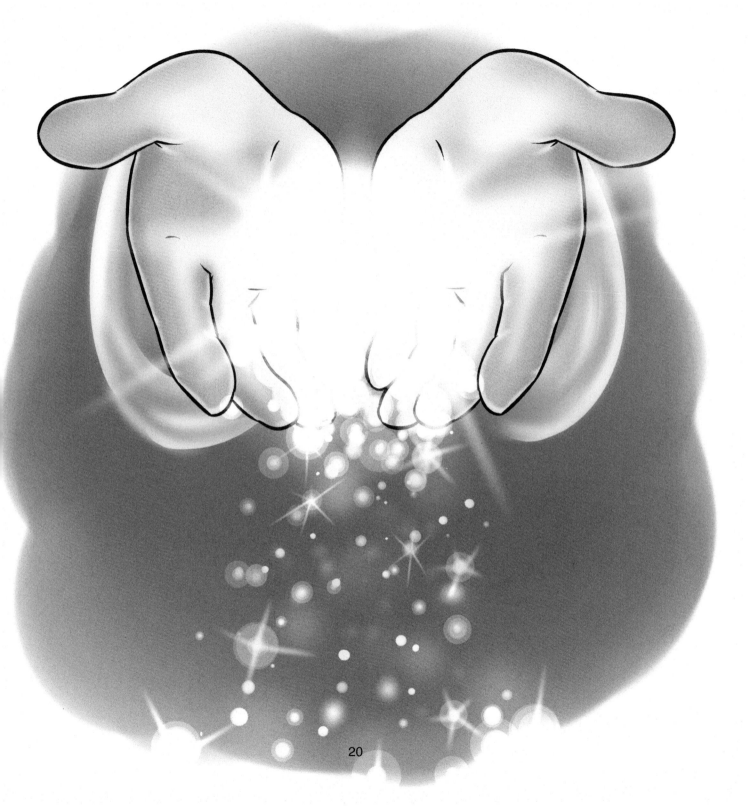

Everywhere that you may go

Everything that you may do

May God go with you

And may God see you through

Be always of good hope

Be always of good cheer

May God always be with you

This will always be our prayer

About the Authors

Dale and Rachael Anthony live in Long Island, New York. Dale is the author of King Liar, a fiction novel set in the oil field.

CPSIA information can be obtained
at www.ICGtesting.com
Printed in the USA
LVOW06*0902290617
539583LV00008B/24/P